Horse
and the Little Girl

HARRY

Written and illustrated by **Jerrold E. Johnson**

To order additional copies of this book, contact:
Xlibris
844-714-8691
www.Xlibris.com
Orders@Xlibris.com

ISBN: 978-1-4257-3136-6 (sc)
ISBN: 978-1-4257-3137-3 (hc)

Library of Congress Control Number: 2006909770

Print information available on the last page

Rev. date: 04/23/2021

Dedicated to

Kayla, Lynnsey, Scott, Matthew, Bridger,
Bryce, Emily, and Andrew Johnson
in memory of Kathryn "Katie" Marie Johnson.God is love. 1

John 4.16

Thanks:

To my son Derek Johnson, Katie's dad, for giving me the go ahead to publish this book by asking me when I was going to do it.

To my wife Margaret for her love, suggestions and editing through tears. To my daughter-in-law Paula who read the original writing to Kayla, Lynnsey and Scott when they were preschool and found them able to appreciate it. To my son Graver for helping me get this stuff on a computer disc to submit for publication.

To Marilyn Jacobs who typed my first manuscript and other essays just because she is a good friend.

To artist friend Susan Blackwood who gave me good critiques, help, and encouragement with my illustrations.

To Valerie Harms for giving me information on options for publishing. And to all my good family and friends who have given me kudos on my writing and have suggested I publish.

JEJ

Published by: Xlibris

These days the small rocking horse stands quietly in the corner. Horse, for that's what she called him, appears lost in thought. It's hard to tell from his face, but if it's true what's been said, "love makes things live", then surely he mourns the gentle little girl with the big smile whose soft brown hair was forever tumbling over her eyes. Those pretty gray-green eyes sparkled every time she saw him. It was she who discovered Horse when she followed Grandma upstairs one day. The girl inspired his renewal and kept him in her prayers, but she is gone now—she lives with God.

Time passes pleasantly enough, with the majestic hall clock grandly chiming the hours. There is, however, a bittersweet quality to the days since the little girl's death that Horse is unable to shake. He dozes a lot and chats with his friends, but over and over again he looks back on his life and tries to make sense of it all, if ever that's possible to do.

Horse is comfortable in the cheerful family
room with a red brick fireplace, much like the one
in the hill house some 30 years before—a happy
memory from the distant past. He is quite old
now and, having always been a bit stiff, delights in

soaking up the warm sunlight streaming through the window. Most evenings he spends with the girl's grandparents, who can be found in their recliners, reading, talking, and napping. Cold nights a friendly fire makes it all very cozy.

Horse's companions are the regal brass goose on the hearth, and a child's maple rocking chair which belongs to the little girl's grandma. A new friend is a cuddly stuffed moose called "Moose", a gift from Grandma to Grandpa. Moose is just the right size for the rocking chair who is much the oldest and very wise from years of quietly observing four generations of family. The goose was a bit stuffy at first. She was quite taken with her importance and let everyone know it. The practical little rocking chair soon set Madam Goose straight. She scolded, "You may be elegant with all your shiny brass, but Horse and Moose and I were made to bring small children happiness." Horse, by nature innocent, didn't notice Goose was being uppity; he's just glad to have company. Horse is pleased that he can see the bookshelf because pictures of the little girl and her cousins smile down on him. Somehow, just seeing them makes him feel better.

Daydreaming, Horse recalls many years ago when he was a gift to the girl's dad from his grandparents. The grandfather was a cowboy in Montana. This made the small horse seem even more special. It was the first genuine "know what's going on" Christmas for the boy and a girl cousin who shared in the fun—truly a happy holiday.

Carols, cookies, angels and a beautiful tree full of lights and ornaments added to the celebration. All the gifts excited the boy but Horse, who was called Harry then, was center ring. It must be so because in the years to follow he found his way into many family pictures, often with a child or two on his back, sometimes showing part of a rocker or his tail and always in the living room with the red brick fireplace. It was a splendid life!

As hobby horses go, Horse wasn't very sturdy even when he was new. No fancy springs like now-a-days. His rockers were too short so the boy's father nailed an extension on one side because the little guy somersaulted over Horse's head from rocking so hard. Despite his frail, pressed cardboard body attached to rickety legs, Horse served the boy and his younger brothers and sister faithfully.

One day, when the children grew too big to ride, Horse was put in a storeroom where he was to spend the next 20 years reflecting on those good times. Horse was lonely. It was tiresome standing in a room with things people collect, never to use again. The many old books were full of exciting tales of adventure, but they kept them secret behind closed covers. His only real pals were a group of stuffed toys all rag tag and threadbare. One was a terry cloth dog with a red tongue. As a toddler the boy bit off, swallowed, coughed it up and scared his mother near to death thinking it was blood. Other friends were his master's brown teddy bear with yellow ears, a floppy deer whose head was so big she couldn't hold it up, a jolly fat blue velveteen pig and Raggedy Ann. Musing about happier days helped, but all in all the future looked bleak. Now and then the boy's parents and youngest brother visited the storeroom. The toys would get excited, but nothing happened so they gave up hope. It was a glum crew—no one seemed to care any more.

One spring day a number of years later the people sold their home and moved far away to where the little girl and her parents lived. Many things were given away. The rest was packed on a big truck called a moving van. For old times sake the little girl's grandmother kept Horse and his friends. It's a wonder why, for Horse's paint was scuffed and faded, his staples loose and missing, ears raw cardboard, pieces broken from his hooves, legs wobbly, and his handle long gone. All told he was a shabby, broken down nag.

Horse was down right ashamed when the tot first saw him, but she didn't mind at all— she thought he was pretty cool. Problem was the small girl was already losing her balance from her disease and Horse, shaky and without his handle, was hard to ride. All the little girl could do was look, grin, and gleefully squeal, "Horse!" (with an emphasis on "s" as best one could tell). Whenever she visited she looked for Horse and, with help, would sit on him and rock.

One day she came and went searching for him. He was nowhere to be found. The girl was perplexed but Grandma quickly found something to distract her in a way that only grandmas can. Grandpa had Horse all in pieces in the garage. Horse was afraid although the man was very gentle. The old man is a people doctor, not a horse doctor, but he was sure he could get Horse all fixed up again. Unfortunately, without proper tools, the going was slow. Eventually, with dogged determination and a lot of love for the little girl, Horse sported new legs. The old doc reinforced his body, extended his rockers, taped his seams, put in a new handle and gave him a new coat of paint. Horse was so thrilled he could hardly stand still. Grandpa thought for a moment he heard an eager whinny. "No, it can't be," he muttered, "I must be hearing things." Uppermost in Horse's mind was to see the little girl and feel her weight in his saddle again. Grandpa was excited too!

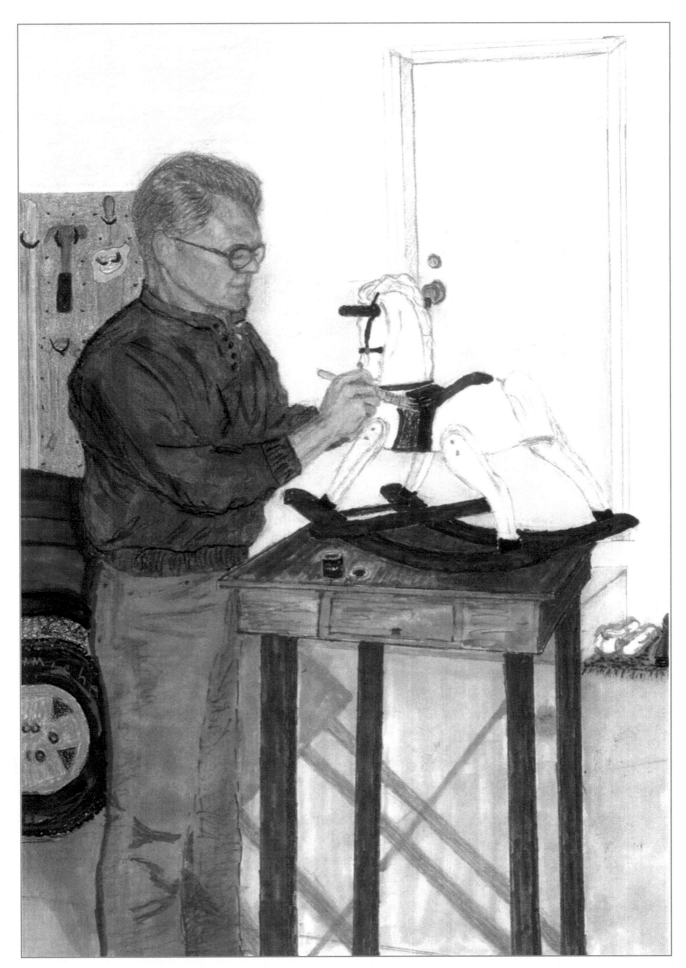

The very next Sunday the little girl and her parents stopped to visit. Horse still didn't recognize the mother although she was very nice. Something about her father stirred Horse's memory which, until now, had eluded him. It was when the large and gentle man lifted her on Horse's back that he realized why he was so familiar. The man was the same little boy who loved him so much and rode him so fearlessly years before. Horse's heart nearly burst with joy. His blue eyes shone, his muscular neck and his tail arched proudly—he near pranced off his rockers. Horse was happy. He knew he was loved and needed once more.

She never rode Horse again. The little girl who loved him so much had weakened rapidly and now was helpless from her disease, her world shrinking by the day. Her dad and grandfather, both doctors, were powerless to help. All the family could do was love and care for her. Early one summer morning she died peacefully in her sleep at home holding her blanket and Puff-a-Lump, her baby stuffed bear.

Suddenly the home filled with family who came to the little girl's funeral. It was all quite confusing to Horse for there was both laughter and tears. He couldn't know that when people lose a loved one, happiness comes from the shared good memories. Tears flowed from the intense sorrow of not being able to hug or talk or play with the little girl again. A new word, "Heaven", was spoken and that she had gone to live there with someone named God. From what Horse could tell it sounded great; a place where children could laugh and play and ride rocking horses all day. Horse thought he'd like that, especially with the little girl there. She'd liven things up. All this thinking made horse's head hurt. It finally dawned on him that these grown-ups were the children who rode him when his mistress' dad grew too big. The small children were the girl's cousins. Everyone wanted to see Horse. After they admired his new look, Grandpa took him back to the bedroom so that in all the commotion he wouldn't be hurt.

Late that night the house was still except for the resonant gongs of the great clock and the mysterious night sounds children listen for in hushed silence as they snuggle deep under the covers. Horse roused from fitful sleep to overhear the grandparents talking softly.

"I feel bad that I was so slow fixing Horse," whispered Grandpa, "but she went down hill so fast. Somehow working on him was like treating an old friend and patient. It's almost as though he knows what's happening, that he misses her too. In my grief it's easy to imagine seeing tears in Horse's eyes."

"Well," said Grandma, "no doubt it was looking through your tears that caused you to feel so.""It's OK," she added, "old things like Horse become so much part of the family they take on a life of their own." She smiled sadly. "One of the blessings of childhood is make believe; at our age they'd say we are silly."

"True," he said thoughtfully, "but maybe make believe is not all that different from belief. Both are a work of the mind. Faith, after all, is a leap into the unknown. We believe in God, we pray to God, yet we really don't see God. We feel God's presence when we see love in action, when people help each other, when they feed the hungry, comfort the sick, smile and say a kind word. We see God when kids clean their rooms, share with brothers and sisters and friends, help their parents and see fun in it all. How easy it would be to be angry and blame God and wonder why God didn't cure our granddaughter," he murmured, "but God doesn't work that way. Death comes to everyone, good and bad, young children and old people, often when least expected. It's especially hard when it's a little child. God is the first to cry."

They agreed God's power is love. Like a strong father he guides us, sustains us, and is there to catch us when we fall. Like a caring mother, she cries and laughs with us, hurts when we hurt, and offers us a soft bosom and gentle arms to comfort and hold us close. Grandma added that God suffers deeply with the family and Horse. Of one thing they were sure the little girl's brief time with them was so special that it was worth all the tears, all the pain.

Grandpa went on to say, "Sometimes our dreams and prayers don't work as we want. We must cherish the good memories—we must learn to celebrate the lives we have and those of whom we love no matter how short—if we do, it won't have been in vain."

Sleep was hard to come by—Horse pondered all this far into the night.

The house is quiet now, the family members have gone their separate ways. Horse is back in the room with the red brick fireplace. He's not sure he understands about all that's happened. He knows for sure he's lonesome, that he aches in his heart. He still stands quietly in the corner but there is a change—a sense of strength and dignity in his bearing that wasn't there before. Horse misses his little friend deeply, however he knows it was her love that made him whole again.

Several weeks passed. Weary from long journeys across the summer sky, old man Sun rose lower and later each morning making possible the cool brisk nights and warm colorful September days. The awful pain of losing the little girl had begun to dull except for those unguarded moments when the urge to cry out became almost unbearable. Horse dreaded those days.

The tot's parents visited as before. Now they carried a small bundle with something wiggly inside. Horse was curious. On one of the visits

the pretty lady opened the blankets on the floor.
Horse could see a baby boy vigorously waving his
arms and kicking his feet.

"Why this must be my friend's brother," thought
Horse. "Well, he's not pretty like her, but he does
have a nice smile and a dimple in each cheek.
And those big hands; I'll bet he will be able to
hold on and ride hard like his dad did." A sense of
hope welled up in Horse's chest. He would have a
new master to ride him again.

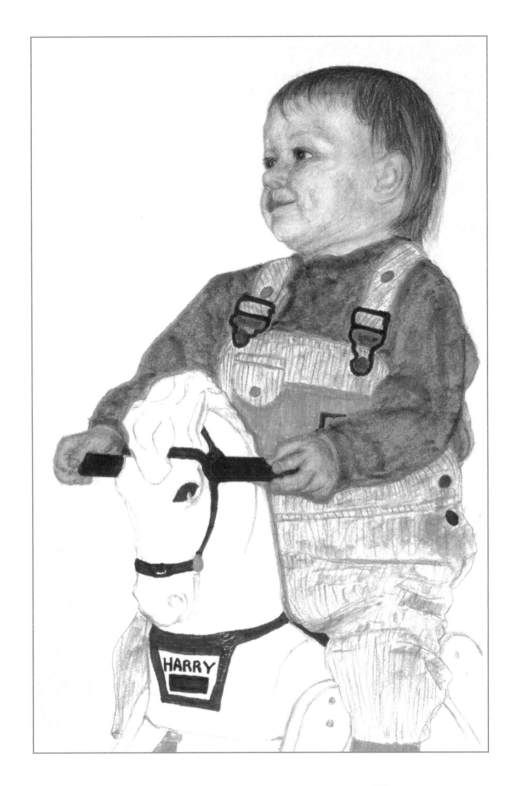

For a moment Horse felt disloyal, "What would my friend the little girl think?" Horse struggled with the problem. Then, with a lump in his throat, he realized he could never have his mistress back. Horse was sure she would want him to be the boy's horse, that to be the best rocking horse he could be was the finest tribute he could give the little girl. Horse knew that her love had given him a new heart, big enough for both children with plenty of room to spare. Grandpa glanced at Horse just then. Perhaps it was the light; it's really hard to say, but he thought he saw a tear in Horse's eye. That was not all. The old man was sure a smile flickered on Horse's lips. "Why those are happy tears," he mused. Then, smiling to himself, Grandpa gave Horse a knowing wink.

The End

Printed in the United States
by Baker & Taylor Publisher Services